# Moving House

## Activity Book

Name _____

Age _____

Class _____

# OXFORD
UNIVERSITY PRESS

Great Clarendon Street, Oxford OX2 6DP

Oxford University Press is a department of the University of Oxford.
It furthers the University's objective of excellence in research, scholarship,
and education by publishing worldwide in

Oxford  New York

Auckland  Bangkok  Buenos Aires  Cape Town  Chennai
Dar es Salaam  Delhi  Hong Kong  Istanbul  Karachi  Kolkata
Kuala Lumpur  Madrid  Melbourne  Mexico City  Mumbai
Nairobi  São Paulo  Shanghai  Taipei  Tokyo  Toronto

OXFORD and OXFORD ENGLISH are registered trade marks of
Oxford University Press in the UK and in certain other countries

© Oxford University Press 2005

The moral rights of the author have been asserted

Database right Oxford University Press (maker)

First published 2005

2009  2008  2007  2006  2005
10 9 8 7 6 5 4 3 2 1

**No unauthorized photocopying**

All rights reserved. No part of this publication may be reproduced,
stored in a retrieval system, or transmitted, in any form or by any means,
without the prior permission in writing of Oxford University Press,
or as expressly permitted by law, or under terms agreed with the appropriate
reprographics rights organization. Enquiries concerning reproduction
outside the scope of the above should be sent to the ELT Rights Department,
Oxford University Press, at the address above

You must not circulate this book in any other binding or cover
and you must impose this same condition on any acquirer

Any websites referred to in this publication are in the public domain and
their addresses are provided by Oxford University Press for information only.
Oxford University Press disclaims any responsibility for the content

ISBN 13: 978 0 19 440141 8
ISBN 10: 0 19 440141 3

Printed in China

*Activities by:* Rebecca Brooke
*Illustrations by:* Ingela Peterson
*Original story by:* Di Taylor

Before reading

# Connect.

Anna

box

truck

man

house

tree

Before reading

# Connect.

doll

TV

table

chair

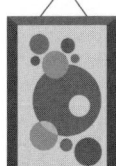

door

picture

# Circle.

**①** This is a cat.

**②** This is a pencil.

**③** This is a man.

**④** This is a CD.

# Pages 2–9

## Write.

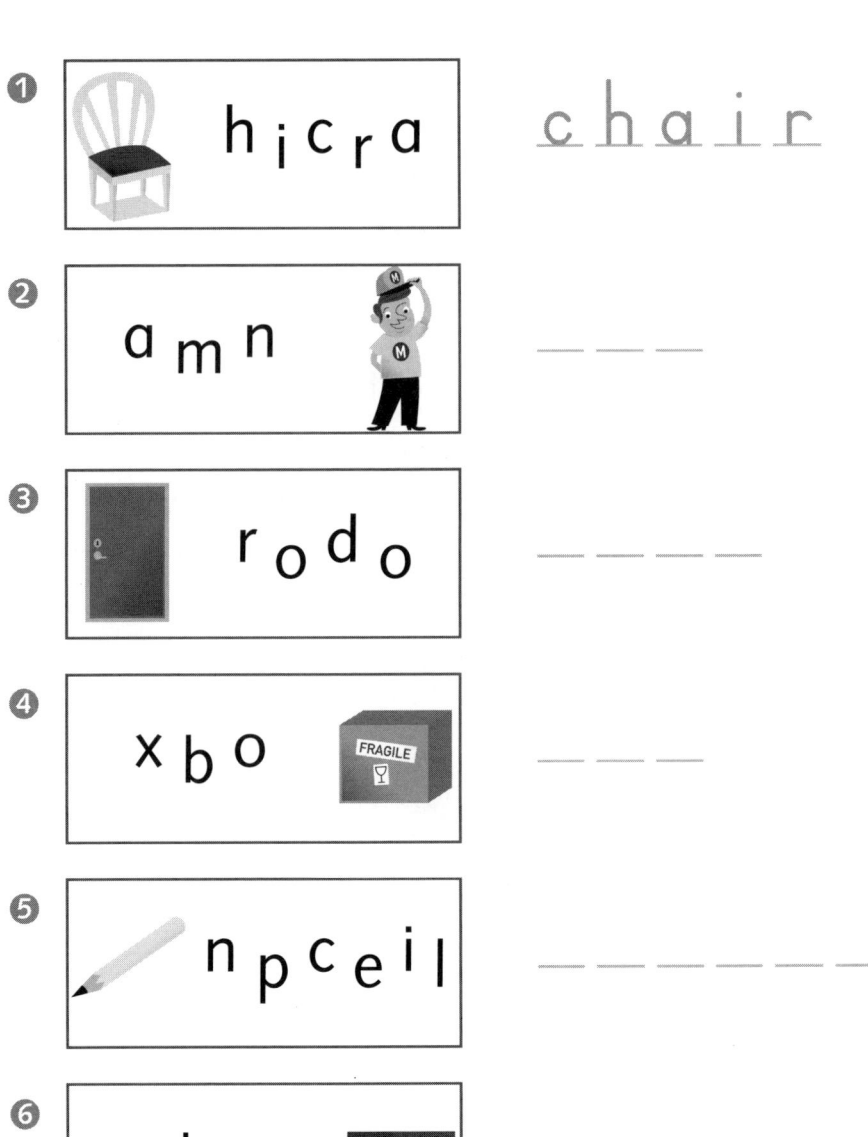

1. hicra — chair
2. amn — ___
3. rodo — ___
4. xbo — ___
5. npceil — ___
6. rktuc — ___

Page 9

# Write.

one   three   four   five   six

1. I can see ___four___ boxes.

2. I can see _____ TVs.

3. I can see _____ cat.

4. I can see _____ pencils.

5. I can see _____ chairs.

6. I can see _____ CDs.

Pages 4–11

# Act the story.

**Dad** The truck is here. Look.
**Anna** No.
**Chant** Anna is unhappy.

**Man** Hello.
**Anna** Goodbye.
**Chant** Anna is unhappy.

**Man** Can I take this?
**Anna** No. That is my TV.
**Chant** Anna is unhappy.

**Man** Can I take this?
**Anna** No. That is my doll.
**Chant** Anna is unhappy.

# Page 11

## Write.

> unhappy   cat   book
> pencil   yo-yo   doll

① Anna has a brown ___cat___.

② Anna has a happy _____.

③ Anna has a pink _____.

④ Anna has a red _____.

⑤ Anna has a yellow _____.

⑥ Anna is _____.

Pages 6–13

# Circle.

1. Anna is moving...
   (house) dog truck

2. The new house is...
   big small yellow

3. The new house has one...
   tree door box

4. The new house is...
   small white happy

5. The new house has two...
   truck doors trees

Pages 2–13

## Connect.

Anna has a cat.

Anna is happy.

Anna is unhappy.

The new house is big.

This is Mom.

This is Dad.

 1
 2
 3
 4
 5
 6

Pages 2–13

# Write.

> doll    house    truck
> green    white    red

1. Anna has a ___doll___.

2. Anna is moving _____.

3. The man has a _____.

4. The trees are _____.

5. The new house is _____.

6. The truck is _____.

Pages 4–13

## Circle yes or no.

1. Anna is a boy.                yes (no)
2. Anna has a dog.               yes  no
3. Anna has a TV.                yes  no
4. Anna has a yo-yo.             yes  no
5. The new house is small.       yes  no
6. The new house is white.       yes  no
7. The man has a truck.          yes  no
8. The man has a hat.            yes  no

Page 14

**Circle** yes **or** no .

1. Anna is unhappy.  yes (no)
2. Anna is happy now.  yes  no
3. Mom is happy.  yes  no
4. Dad is unhappy.  yes  no
5. Anna likes the new house.  yes  no
6. The boxes are in the truck.  yes  no
7. The boxes are in the house.  yes  no
8. Anna is in the truck.  yes  no

# After reading

## Look and write.

After reading

## Chant the story.

Anna is moving house today.
Here is the truck.
The man says, Hello.
Anna says, Goodbye.
Stop. That is my TV.
Stop. That is my doll.
Anna sees the new house.
The new house is big.
The new house is white.
The trees are green.
Anna likes the new house.
Anna is happy. Let's go.